Finishing What We Started

Return to Kenya, 2016

Dalen Garris

This is a work of history. Historical individuals and places and events are mentioned.

Published by Revivalfire Ministries

ISBN 13:

For information, address
dale@revivalfire.org

First paperback printing September, 2020

Printed in the United States of America

Introduction

I started this trip as a sort of maintenance effort. I had first come to Kenya twelve years earlier and wanted to know how the churches were still doing. This is what Paul did – go back and make sure they are still on fire.

I started at one end of Kenya and travelled the distance to the other side. Everywhere we went, we met an unsatiated hunger for God. Not just for the idea of God or a new form of worship, but for a deep and enduring personal experience with the Spirit of God. They were starving.

It's hard to say, but I got the very distinct impression that He was just as hungry for them as they were for Him. I say that because wherever we went we were met with the powerful presence of God. These were His precious children, and He was in love with them.

There is a drawing power to the Holy Spirit that extends past physical barriers. We would be way out in the Bush and people would come from everywhere. The power of God drew them in. God is moving here.

This was supposed to be a finishing of my previous trips to Kenya. I have a feeling it was more of a new beginning.

Table of Contents

20. Small Stuff

Sometimes I wonder what it would be like to be able to see all the invisible things that go on in the spiritual world. You know there is activity there by all the crazy things that happen on this side of the veil. You just can't see them.

For instance, every time I head out for another round of revival meetings in Africa, all hell breaks loose. As soon as I purchase the tickets, we start battling some of the weirdest stuff you have ever heard of. It has gotten so bad that the owner of the computer store that fixes our computers started laughing at me this time. "Nope, I've never seen this problem before with anyone else. You must be heading out on another trip, aren't you?"

I always used to figure that the more intense the battles were, the greater the mission was going to be. I'm not sure that's necessarily true anymore. I think it's just gotten to be routine for the devil to go into high gear whenever he sees the next itinerary come up. Old habits die hard.

This trip hasn't been any different. This time, the trouble followed us all the way to Nairobi, but usually, everything smoothes out as we get into gear. We still have battles, but it is as if everything shifts, and the old crew of demons is dismissed while the next crew takes over.

You think I'm kidding, but there is a definite

difference in the kinds of things that happen once the campaign has begun. Before I leave the States, everything just seems to be designed to drive us crazy. Once the campaign has started, however, trouble happens all around me, even to those who are helping us in the campaign but not to me. It's as if I am in a bubble while a war rages around me.

Does it happen like that all the time? No, but it happens enough to form a definite pattern. And enough to make you wonder what is really going on in the invisible world of the spiritual realm. Are there generals and privates in Satan's armies? Do they map out battle plans, send out spies and special ops? Do they have pictures of us posted on their Post Office wall as the 10 Most Wanted? What is really going on behind the scenes?

I don't know. God never put any graphic descriptions in His Word for us to ponder on other than to admonish us to put on the whole armor of God because Satan is like a roaring lion seeking whom he can devour and that he would be loosed on the earth in the last days. I guess that's small stuff for Him.

Instead, God has pointed us to focus on having mercy on the lost who do not know Jesus and who have never known the freedom of salvation. Our job is to push through the smoke and fire and hold up the Great Commission as our battle cry. Let God be our rear guard to cover us as we take the battle to the enemy to hold up the Blood-Stained Banner and claim victory. That's the big stuff.

No, it's not easy. I don't know what is going on in the subterranean world. I guess we'll see it all when we finally pass through the veil. In the meantime, however, we have the weapons of prayer to bring to bear upon the enemy.

The rest is just small stuff.

First Days of Fire

Well, we are two days down, and a whole bunch yet to go. So far so good.

Services both yesterday and today were … um … I'm trying to choose between "electrifying" and "wild". It depends on which side of the Atlantic you are from.

Ricci, the young man who is traveling with me, is looking wild-eyed at what he is seeing. He expected the song service to be lively. He has come from a Pentecostal background, his family is intimately involved in the Brownsville revival, so he knows what it is to have the Spirit of God fall on a service. This was much more than he had ever experienced, but he was at least prepared for it.

To the folks here in Africa, it was simply an anointing of the Holy Spirit. This is Africa, and they know how to praise the Lord here with everything they have. And everything they have, they give to their worship in singing, dancing, and praise. To many of us sedate Americans, it would seem wild, but for them, it is just God.

But it was the closing prayer that Ricci was not prepared for.

After the message was done, instead of praying with the congregation, I handed it over to Pastor Kibedi. (Actually, it is now, Archbishop Kibedi. He has grown immensely in God during the last 12 years that I have known him.)

Kibedi started praying ... and praying ... and praying. As the intensity grew the passion started to rise and spread throughout the entire church. The closing prayer became 45 minutes of fire. People were praying at the top of their lungs, crying and calling out to God with everything in them.

For them, this was transforming; for Ricci this was wild! You just don't see anything like this in

America. Too bad for us.

It would be easy to think that this was just "wildfire" – all emotion and bluster – but after 12 years out here, I have learned that while this might be too much for our polished services in America, this is very real for Africans. They deal with God on a very different level than we do.

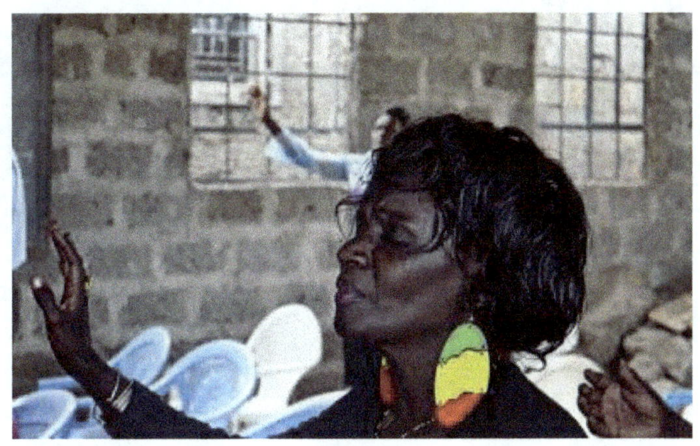

As the service ended, several answered the call, crying and weeping for individual repentance, rededication, and healing. Their hearts had been deeply broken and affected. God is their Father, and they are so softhearted toward God that they cling desperately to their deep, personal relationship with Him.

This is the stuff that I live for. This is the real

Gospel at work. Call it crazy; I call it God.

We have a way to go. Ricci will see this many times before we board the plane for home. It may seem wild to him now, but I have a feeling he will look at it more as the supernatural anointing of the Holy Spirit by the time we are done.

And then, like myself, he will have to figure out how to explain what this is like to the folks back home. Good luck on that one, Ricci.

Casting Out Demons

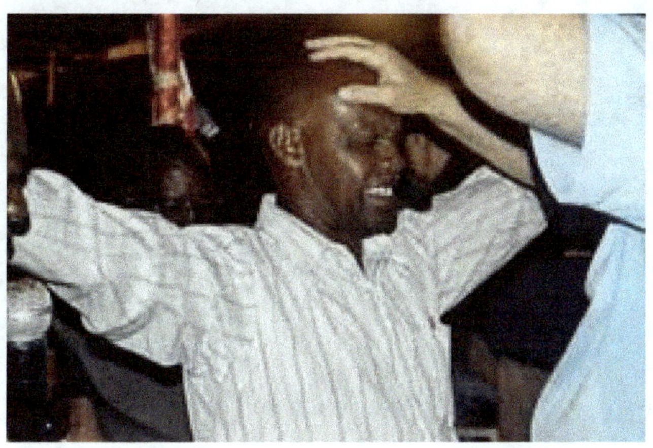

The air here hangs heavy, like a wet woolen blanket. It's barely noticeable except in that dragging lethargy that you feel all day. I don't know if that's what it is or just the hangover of jet lag that stubbornly hangs on to wake you up in the middle of the night and then drag you down in the middle of the day. Hopefully, it will get better as we get acclimated to either the time zone or the African humidity.

I've done 7 services in 5 days. I have 42 days of services ahead of me with one day for a break. While the intensity can be exhausting, the curious thing is that I seem to fill back up again quickly. I hope that continues to be the case as we get through this trip.

Last night we cast the devil out of one young lady. Another girl had fits, but I think that was mostly from an overworked emotional response. But not this other woman.

Often, whenever the Spirit is falling heavy during a service, the congregation wants to get prayed over – healings, greater dedication, faith, sin, a husband, and whatever else is oppressing their lives. The hearts of these people are very soft, and their needs are great, so they possess a deep desire to be in communion with their Father. Failure, sin, and separation break their hearts. Whenever they can feel the presence of the Holy

Spirit's anointing, they want to take advantage of it.

So, we had a prayer line.

I went down the line, and it was all the usual requests. Their deep sincerity touches my heart and makes me pray all the harder for them. There is also a feeling like oil flowing through you into them. It's faint but unmistakable. I'll tell you what, if it is just my imagination, then it sure is a good imagination!

The one lady started winding up as I laid hands on her, and in a short while, she couldn't contain it. It took three women and me to calm her down.

But then came the lady at the end of the line.

Something about her made me feel like she was going to explode. I just knew it. Sure enough, as soon as the oil on my hands touched her, she turned into a wild woman. BUT – and this is telling – she wouldn't (or couldn't) take her head away from my hand. She twisted, and contorted, and turned all around, but always my hand remained on her forehead. There was more going on here than some emotional overload.

As I was commanding the spirit to come out and pleading the blood of Jesus against it, it turned and looked at me through her eyes and growled, "I'm not coming out! I'm NOT coming out!" Let me tell you, it is an eerie feeling when a demonic spirit speaks right to you.

That was it for me. I put my face right in front of her and said, "You know who I am. YOU KNOW WHO I AM! And you know the authority I have over you. GET OUT! NOW!"

And it did.

She was delivered in a moment. Immediately I made her start praising and thanking the Lord. There is power in praise, and it is a healthy antidote against any loose spirits that would try to come back in. A feeling of peace settled down on us like snow. It was done.

Services aren't always that wild, but then again, this is Africa, and anything can happen. But as they say here in Kenya, "Hakuna Matata" – "no worries". Thank God we have a Savior that we can go to with whom deliverance such as this is freely available.

Small Things

It's been a week and a half, and we've been to 6 churches so far. All of them have been poor churches – dirt floor, tin roof held up by sticks, no windows or doors. One church we were at was nothing more than a ragged, sun-worn tarp over a steel frame. This is by no means some glorious crusade with lights and accolades and glamour. This is the gospel at its most basic level.

Going into the morning service on Easter morning, there was only 4 or 5 women with some kids and a couple of men in the church … and about 20 empty plastic chairs. Lord, is this where I am really supposed to be? Have I made a mistake in coming here? All this trouble, effort, sacrifice, and money to come here, and this is it? I am not looking for fame and glory, but honestly, shouldn't I be ministering to more than this?

I've asked this question many times before. And I don't always get an answer. But I am reminded that God uses the small, foolish things to confound the wise. Peter's meeting with Cornelius in Acts 10 was pretty small too, but it opened up the dispensation to the Gentiles – no small matter.

Still, we would all like to see results that are powerful and earthshaking for our efforts. But God doesn't do things that way. May God bless all those great big churches with all their grand services with thousands of people, but somebody has to come down here and minister to the poorest and most precious of His saints. So here I am.

I once told God I would take the jobs that no one else wanted. I guess He heard me.

So, I sucked it up and went inside.

When I preach, the only thing I can see is the message that I am preaching. I just can't focus on anything else. So, I didn't notice as the place filled up. But I did know we were on fire!

I don't know where everyone came from. They must've just drifted in as I was preaching. It no longer mattered. God was there – not by wishful thinking or theological conjecture, but in power and in spirit. The anointing was there to lift every one of us into the Spirit. Happy Easter. God showed up.

On Monday, we took the message into the Rueben slums of Nairobi. I won't show you the worst pictures -- they are that bad. But guess what? That's where Jesus asks us to go. Like the lowly Nazarene, searching for souls amongst the dregs of society, amongst the most needy, sick, and poor, and in slums like this, this is where you find the real

Gospel at work.

Somehow God uses stuff like this to enact great moves of God. I have no idea how. It makes no sense to me to sacrifice and spend so much to come to such tiny places with such little people that are so poor, but I said I would do it. And I have kept my Word. I expect Him to keep His also.

"For who hath despised the day of small things?" Zechariah 4:10

Finishing Nairobi

I am finally done with Nairobi. We did 7 or 8 churches and I don't know how many services. I can tell I'm tired because I can't think. Everything feels like molasses. I'll be driving and not know where I'm going, and I'm always tired. Between dirt, the traffic jams, the mosquitoes, and the humidity, I am ready to get out of the city and into the countryside so I can get some rest.

We've been staying in a tiny hotel on the gritty side of Nairobi. We are the only guests here. I'm not sure how they pay the bills, but it is nice to have the whole place to ourselves, including the cook. But it would be nice to get out of this tiny shoebox of a room.

All the meetings were good. I revisited some churches that I had not been to in a decade, and they still remembered and were excited to see me. That was a very reassuring feeling.

Sometimes you wonder. I put in a whole lot to bring this message to hundreds of small churches scattered like seed all over the country. Besides the money and effort, the sacrifice of time that could have been spent with my girls as they were growing up is the hardest thing that I had to give. In the end, however, there is no doubt in me that God has sent me in this manner to these places. This is how He always does it – not to the big shots, but to the foolish things of the world so that God alone gets the glory.

In one of these small churches some 8 to 10 years ago, I prayed over a woman who was deathly sick and healed her. Today, she is a pastor in one of the churches here. They have not forgotten. Big things can happen in small places.

In many places, they have seen the things that I told them years ago come to pass. In other places, they have seen exponential growth because of the message I delivered to them. They still remember.

There are still five weeks to go. Tomorrow, we head for the interior and then down into the arid bush country of the south. I have Ricci, a young friend of mine, with me. He is about to have an incredible experience these next few weeks that will change his life. It will be something he will remember for a long time.

If nothing else, that alone will be worth it.

Land of Goshen

The air is cool and fresh out here. We are a couple of hours north of Nairobi near Mt. Kenya. What a change in the atmosphere it is here. Where Nairobi is dirty and gritty with too many people crawling all over the place, this place is cool, fresh, and open, like something out of a commercial for laundry detergent.

We are at the Goshen Farm Resort. It is off-season, the beginning of the rainy season, so the hotel they have brought us to is empty except for us. We are engulfed in lush foliage of flowers, succulents, and bushes. Some of the colors are so bright they hurt your eyes to stare at. It's like the garden in some English manor out in a lush countryside. No internet, but who cares?

I have two churches to preach at during these three days. The first is Bishop Maina's church. I have been here before with my daughters about seven years ago. Not much has changed since then and they still remember me.

The other church is a new one for me, but they have heard about this American who doesn't preach like other Americans, and they want to hear what I have to say. I can tell they are a little hesitant, but they hand me a short 30-minute service first early on Sunday morning. I gave them what I got, and they were on their feet by the time we were done. I guess that means I passed the test.

The main service was a riot of singing and dancing that was infectious. I usually sit through the song services so I can get focused on the message I am about to bring. (Actually, I'm sitting down to give my legs a break because I'll be on my feet for the next hour.) But not today. When the praise and worship are this good, you can't sit down. How I wish I could capture this in a bottle and bring it back home! Ricci captured it on video, so that may be the next best thing.

The third service of the day was back at Bishop Maina's. When we got there, the place was packed. Apparently, the word had spread and pastors from several churches had come to hear this message. We had a question-and-answer session that lasted two hours, and still, no one wanted to leave.

I have had many meetings like this. They understand the message and hang on to every word I speak, their fervor is through the roof, and they are excited to take your words and put them into action. You have done your job – you have planted the seed that God has given you to plant. Now it is time to let go and leave them to the mighty hands of God.

Some seed grows, multiples, and brings forth a hundred-fold; others do not. What happens next is up to them. My job is done here, and I am on to the next field to plant the next set of seeds. But somehow, I get the feeling that this place is going to take the messages I have given them and set their area on fire.

Revival in Namanga

We made it through Nairobi traffic … almost.

A cop stopped us for making an illegal right-hand turn downtown and said he was taking Ricci to court and impounding the vehicle. (Right. And how are you going to make me do that without having a gun on you?) But I played the game and offered to pay the "fine" of 5,000 shillings. Anything, just get out of my car.

After picking up 6 cases of Bibles, we headed for Namanga in the heart of Massailand. (I have never been able to figure out if you spell it Masai or

Massai.) The need for Bibles has always been great down there. One time I gave a case of Bibles to a pastor whose people were illiterate, but they were able to read those Bibles! Talk about an excited pastor!

Another time, I gave Bibles to a church where the pastor was the only one in the entire church that had a Bible, and it was ragged and falling apart. His people would walk through the dark in the bush where lions roamed to come and take turns reading … just so they could feel how good it was to read the Word of God. Boy, that kind of stuff just flat out gets to you. I gave them some Massai Bibles and a Proclaimer, an audio Bible in the Massai language. Wow, did that rock their world to hear the Gospel of John coming out of that box in their own language!

So, this time, I got them a couple of cases of Massai and some Swahili. But no matter how many I bring, there is never enough. At least we have some to give out as seed that will bring back a harvest.

Pastor Samuel is the young pastor here. He was here the very first time I came almost 10 years ago. He told me that the small churches that I had visited out in the bush on my previous trips have all experienced revival and have now all become big churches -- real revival, he says, the kind that has sent a wave of excitement through Massailand.

There must be something to what he says because our meetings here today were packed. Pastors have come from miles around to hear me talk about revival. While I may not exactly be famous, they have heard of me and want to hear more. They are hungry for a move of God.

The services were incredible. I preached for an hour and a half in the afternoon and again in the evening. Instead of one of us leading them in the closing prayer, I closed by asking them to pray. Wow. They peeled the paint off Heaven's doors! Twenty or thirty minutes later, they settled down so

I could pray over some of them for salvation and healing.

This was a night to remember, for both them and us. God did something here. I'm not sure what, but then, when have I ever known. Years later, we will look back on this night as the point in time when God birthed something very special in these people.

Maybe even the start of a revival in Namanga.

A Light Amongst the Massai

Mornings are gorgeous here in Namanga. There's a cool, refreshing tropical feeling in the air every morning. And each morning, little spider monkeys come out to entertain us for food. Almost like street kids who dance on street corners for change. They will come and take a banana right out of your hand.

But by mid-morning, they are gone, back up into the mountain that is right behind us. It makes you wonder what other animals are up there. The whole area looks exactly like west Texas – arid scrub brush littered with short hardy trees – but instead of mesquite, these are acacia trees. And instead of Armadillos, they have monkeys, instead of deer, lions.

We had two more services here today. The afternoon service was full, but the evening service was packed again. These people are serious. Both services lasted around 3 hours, but no one wanted to leave. Not even close. They are determined to have what I have promised them is in the Word of God.

The Massai are a very different kind of people. They live secluded lives very close to the land and the animals. Lions fear them and will leave whenever a Massai is near, but the other tribes in Kenya look down on them as almost sub-human and uncivilized. They are almost correct. The Massai are very different, their culture is very dark, and the Massai religion is very demonic. Nevertheless, when they get saved, they get saved hard. Their transformation from darkness to Light is no little thing and they take it much more seriously than most others.

You can tell. These revival meetings have brought people in from the bush because they have seen what this message has done from when I have been here before, and they are desperate to get more.

It's not the excitement or the fervor that makes me feel a difference here amongst the Massai. It is a very different anointing from God that I feel. It is hard to describe on paper, but it is almost as if God is a co-conspirator with me, secretly whispering in my ear to not worry, He's got this. He has brought me here to speak to His people. He has the message and the anointing. All I have to do is show up and open my mouth. He will take it from there.

And He does. What a service! This is just like last night. Something broke open in the heavenlies. I have no idea what, but everyone here can feel it. God has brought them hope. A real vision for God always has to be planted with hope in your heart before it can ever be established by your faith.

That's what He has done. He has given them a Light in the darkness.

Possibilities in Mboni

We were told that the next place I would minister in was Mboni. I have no idea where Mboni is. Mboni is not on the map. And if there is a hotel there, I'm not sure I'll want to stay in it.

So, we were told instead to go to Machakos and call the pastor for directions from there. Now in Machakos, there is a hotel. A nice one. I'm talking about hot showers, real food, A/C, and no mosquitos. Ricci and I are both ready for a break, and the hotel we found gave that to us – a 4-star hotel for Motel 6 prices. Nice.

But the church? It is one hour out into the bush. (groan) So off we go as soon as we can because the people have been there since 10:00 am waiting for us. Really? We had to travel for two-and-a-half hours to get here, check in to the hotel, and then travel for an hour over dirt roads to get to church. Did it not occur to them that we were not going to make it there by 10:00?

Not to worry. Hakuna Matata. They don't care. No white man, especially a white man from America, has ever come out here to preach the Gospel to them. They will wait.

Needless to say, the services were great. The translation was tough because they are not used to an American accent, but they got the message. Especially the part about them being able to change the world.

I had to carefully paint that picture for them first. Here they are, little people, poor, and an hour from anywhere. How can they change the world? But as I explain how God works, and how even the greatest fire can start with a single match, they begin to realize that the process of revival is not dependent on their abilities, position, power or wealth, but that if they can just start a fire here, God can spread it around the world.

I watch as the realization spreads across their faces. *"Not by might, nor by power, but by my spirit, saith the Lord of hosts"* (Zech. 4:6). *"God hath chosen the foolish things of the world to confound the wise;"* (1 Cor. 1:27)

The service the next day was pretty much the same, but this time I ended with a healing/prayer line. I don't do this often because the message is what is important and often it can get lost in the miracles. But I just had this feeling ...

At first, it was just a few. And then they came pouring down to the altar. We in the West do not understand or realize the depth of these people's needs. Like deep waters that seem placid on the surface but hide currents that run underneath, these simple people have needs that only God can touch.

They fill the front of the church, three lines deep. As it happens so often, everyone who gets in line gets healed. Then I came to an old lady who had pain in her legs. I kneeled down to lay hands on her wrinkled, knobby knees and pray. Bang! She is healed. I know this because, not only did I feel the anointing come down, but when I stood up and asked her if she was healed, she began to dance a jig! I'm guessing that means yes.

There were a couple of others with dramatic results, but there was one girl in particular who wanted me to pray for her to serve God. But when I asked her to start praising the Lord, she couldn't. She was locked up tight. A demonic stronghold had taken hold of her, and she couldn't free herself. I could feel the fury and authority of the Lord rise up within me as I rebuked that foul spirit in the blood of Jesus Christ. You could feel a *CRACK!* in the room as I claimed power in God and declared victory in the name of Jesus. And just like that, it was gone.

I don't know what will ultimately happen out here. I believe we opened up a new door for them and exposed them to greater possibilities of faith than they have ever known. They know. They see. They get it. But will they march through that door and claim the promises that God has given them? Will they overcome the constraints of "church" and reach out for revival instead?

I don't know, but I do know that we have planted a seed of hope, faith, and possibility in them, and they can take it as far as they can have the courage to believe.

They can change the world.

Kibwezi, a Dry and Thirsty Land

We are on the road to Tsavo, the area where man-eating lions once terrorized the railway workers many years ago. Ricci is driving while I am writing this because I am way too tired by the time I get back to the hotel each night to write down our experiences. I have to do it on the road.

We just finished two days out in the bush country outside the town of Kibwezi. There is not much rain out here. A dry and gritty red dirt is everywhere, as are the big, fat Baobab trees that have trunks that are ten feet wide with little stubby branches. They remind me of the dinosaur in *Meet the Robinsons* – "great big head; little tiny arms!" There's not much water out here, so the roots of these trees are unbelievably expansive and wide, searching for water in a dry and thirsty land. Sounds like something out of Isaiah.

The church here is a small mud building about 15x30. The walls are red mud packed into a lattice of sticks with the ever-present corrugated iron roof. Dirt floor, no windows, and a makeshift door – this is not your standard, everyday church like we would expect in America. This is the evidence of desperate faith and a desire to worship God where it is not convenient.

I was here with my two girls seven years ago,

and they still remember us. They tell me that I am the only white guy who has ever come out here to bring the gospel. (I have heard that more than a few times.) So yeah, naturally they remember me, but they also remember the Bibles I gave them and the Four Steps to Revival booklets. The pastor held up a copy of the booklet that he has had for 10 years!

They even remember the message I gave seven years ago. The pastor tells me that the church has grown since then and they have come from far to see me. He leans over and says, "They are so thirsty!"

I get choked up at that. All the big evangelists can keep the large auditoriums and huge church services. Let me have these little people out here who are so thirsty that they will walk 10 to 13 hours just to come to hear the Word of God because "they are so thirsty". Are they not the ones that the Lord told us to come to when He said, *"Inasmuch as you have done this to the least of these, you have done it unto me"*? (Matt. 25:40)

Sometimes I wonder how the Lord is going to turn this into a worldwide revival, but He quickly reminds me that He is God, and that's what He does! Not my problem. My job is to show up; His job is to take it from there. All I can do is plant the seed in the dirt; He is the one that brings it to life. *"Who has despised the day of small things?"* (Zech. 4:10)

"The Spirit of the Lord God is upon me; because the Lord hath anointed me to preach good tidings unto the meek;

He hath sent me to bind up the brokenhearted, to proclaim liberty to the captives, and the opening of the prison to them that are bound;

To proclaim the acceptable year of the Lord, and the day of vengeance of our God;

To comfort all that mourn;

To appoint unto them that mourn in Zion, to give unto them beauty for ashes, the oil of joy for mourning, the garment of praise for the spirit of heaviness;

That they might be called trees of righteousness, the planting of the Lord,

That he might be glorified."

(Isaiah 61: 1-3)

Planting Seeds

Where was I? Ah yes, Tsavo, where the man-eating lions were. Not to worry, they're all gone now, replaced by progress, people, and roads. Kenya has changed dramatically in the ten years since I've first been here. I suppose it's for the good, but there were some quaint cultural things that are either gone or commercialized for the western tourists.

The town I landed in is Mwatate (mmwaa-tah-tay). Pastor Evans ministered with me on my very first trip to Africa, 12 years ago. He now has his own church here and it is growing faster than any of the other churches in the area.

I can see why. To say his services are lively would be mild. And wow, can his wife Sophie sing!

From here we drove three hours to Mombasa. I have never been to the church here before. The only other time I came through Mombasa, the pastor forgot to tell his congregation that I was coming, so we had a service with 4 or 5 people and left.

But not this time. The place was packed, and half of it was with pastors from surrounding churches. Again, after two days of meetings, the excitement level was through the roof. They keep promising me that they will do everything I have taught them and will take this gospel to the entire area so that when I come back, I will see the fruit.

Actually, I hear this at every place I go. I am told that there is an anointing that I bring with me when I come that they can feel. I can't feel anything; so honestly, I really don't know what they feel. But after a few hundred times of having heard this from pastors all across Africa, I believe it. God is doing something special with these people – something you can't see with your eyes or understand from the facts you see around you.

The results of that anointing keep presenting themselves. Churches I preached at years ago have now grown exponentially. Pastors have gone into the ministry and established strong churches because of this message. Many of those went out and planted hundreds of churches using the principles in *Four Steps to Revival.* I think God has taken me on this last final tour so I can get a small glimpse of what He is doing and catch a vision of what He is about to do.

After Mombasa, I did a Sunday service in one of the slums of Nairobi, a church I was at a decade ago. And again, we had an explosive service. The supernatural is becoming routine.

I have done about 50 meetings in about 30 days. It has finally caught up with me and knocked me out for a couple of days, but now I am ready to get out of bed and tackle the last leg of this journey.

This may be my final tour. There is a feeling of urgency to press this message of *Four Steps to Revival* upon these people. Like Johnny Appleseed, I can only scatter the seeds; these pastors will have to take it once it has germinated and bring it to harvest. My part in this process will be done.

The Lord has reminded me, however, that the

only seeds of revival that will not grow are the ones that have not been planted. That is enough to get me up and going again.

Feeding the Multitude

After Nakuru, I headed up to Eldoret. Eldoret is a busy city. Imagine all the noise, honking, dust, and clamor of a circus of wild animals and clowns gone wild. That would give you a picture of the downtown streets of Eldoret.

The White Castle Hotel is right in the middle of all this melee. It's the same hotel I stayed at in 2010 when I was here last. At 16 bucks a night, you can imagine what it was like – clean and basic, but a bit Spartan in comfort. But hey, there was hot water in the shower!

Services were on the outskirts of town in a typical African church with corrugated iron roofs and walls. Somebody must have made a fortune selling iron sheets because they are as ubiquitous as dirt across Africa.

The pastor is asking for me to give two services today. While I am not exactly feeling frisky right now, it is hard to say no. These people, like all the others that I have ministered to, are hungry to hear about revival. It is like a dream for them that will lift them out of what they have now.

It's not the poverty or the drab conditions of their lives; neither is it a discontent with their church – it's the dream of reaching through the realities of this life and being able to not only touch God but to immerse themselves in His presence. They need God. And they are looking at me to introduce them to Him in the excitement of revival.

I'm not sure how I'm supposed to think about that. I just keep pressing out this message that God has given me, over and over, place after place, meeting after meeting in close to 800 churches across Africa. No matter how many times I have worried about getting stale and repetitive, it is always new and exciting to them. But for me, I get to have the crowd in my hands for an hour each time and watch their excitement grow as they grasp the message.

And then we passed out the Bibles!

I asked how many have Bibles. I think there were three or four out of the whole crowd. How am I supposed to lead them into battle if they have no swords? How will this message find any traction in their hearts without the Word of God to establish them? What good is "be thou warmed and filled", if you want them to grow into strong warriors in this battle for human souls?

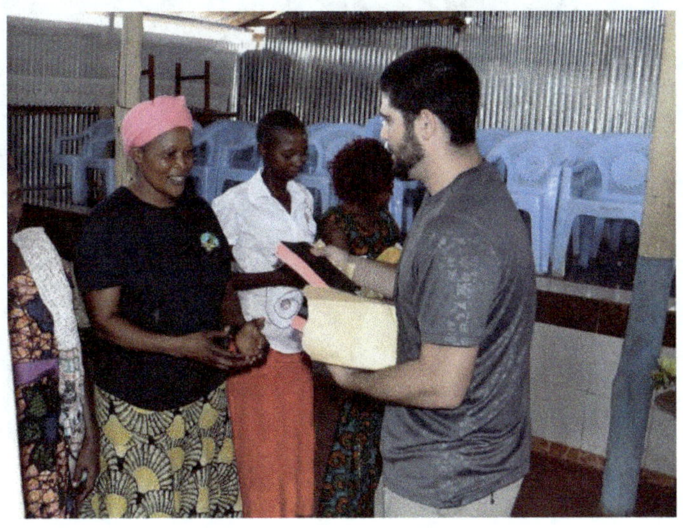

One thing I've learned – you never have enough Bibles. I had given the pastor a case of 34 Bibles, but they got sucked up immediately. So, we dug into a second case, which had been earmarked for another church. Oh well. I guess I'll have to worry about that tomorrow.

Right now, we have some very hungry and insistent people to feed the Bread of Life to.

Rekindling the Fire

Ahhhhhh. Three days off! One to travel from Kitale to Kisumu, and two days to do absolutely nothing! I feel like a rich man with time to squander however I want.

I had the same experience in Kitale as I have had in so many other places. Hungry for God to do something special in their lives, they come expecting a miracle. Because I am not like all the other American preachers, they get something they didn't expect, but once they taste it, they want more.

They expected a soft message of peace and

blessings – which is always nice to hear – but they got one of repentance and price, and they recognize the difference.

I have found that their understanding of scripture and the ways of the Spirit are often more sophisticated than we in the West expect. They get the difference between the old-fashioned gospel from 50 years ago and the modern gospel they are hearing from us now – as evidenced by their exuberant "amens" when I hit certain doctrinal points.

They know the truth; they just need someone to inspire them, and only the Holy Ghost can do that. He is the One they are waiting for. Once the fire is lit, however, get out of the way! It is like standing in a field of wheat that is so dry it has turned white and brittle, striking a match, and then dropping it into the wheat. The results are always explosive.

That is what I am experiencing out here. I am getting phone calls and messages from the places I have just been to over the last month or so telling me that the fire is still burning and that souls getting saved. Nothing unusual about that; the message works. Always has.

As I was leaving Kitale after three days of meetings, I stopped at the Challenge Farm, an orphanage run by Cheri Thompson, an American woman who came out here, fell in love with the kids, and never left. She has turned a dream into a sprawling reality. There are hundreds of kids running all over the place, smiling, playing, studying, and growing up as strong, productive Christians. This woman has accomplished something incredible.

As for me right now, I am trying to turn off all the switches and just coast. My batteries have run dry, and my spark of inspiration is dead. I need to just shut it off for a while until I can catch up to myself again. I have hardly come out of the room for two days. I've already seen Kisumu so what is there to see? I've been to enough restaurants in my time and seen enough sights, so leave me alone. I'm fine right here. (Is this what it is like to get old?)

I have heard from the lady pastor at the church I will be going to tomorrow. They are praying. What else can you say? They are praying. God, she says, is faithful and will direct me to meet the brethren of the Lord who are patiently waiting for me. They are praying.

That's all it takes to rekindle my fire – they are praying. They don't know who I am, but when has that ever mattered? They are waiting for Him. And He will be there.

Bread Upon the Waters

Mornings in Kisumu are fresh and clean in spite of all the dirt that is in the city streets that seems to rise out of the ground during the rush and hubbub of the day. In the early morning, the sidewalk vendors are staking out their sidewalk territories and getting ready for the business of the day as the city slowly rises out of her slumber of the night. I love this time in the morning.

I have just spent the last two days with a very small band of pastors in what seems to be an abandoned schoolroom on the outskirts of the city.

The roads that lead to the meeting place have become mud holes and impassible lakes after the all-night rain we just had. We had to forego a couple of the roads because the water was too deep. As it was, I plowed through a couple of 20-foot-wide puddles that were up to the axles, hoping and praying that I would not get stuck. This is the rainy season, so this is no surprise for me.

Less than a dozen pastors have shown up to hear the message that I am about to bring to them. My friend who is organizing these meetings for me is developing a network of churches across Kenya and these pastors are part of it. Although there are only a few of them, if I can plant a seed deep enough in their hearts and light a fire in them that they will take back to their churches, then it will be worth plowing through the mud. God knows what He is doing, even if He doesn't let the rest of us in on it.

At the end of two days of meetings, they are so excited that they are already planning for a great big conference for me next year. I get this same response from every place that I minister at. Everybody is always so lit up from the message that they all want me to come back the next year. I always I tell them that, no, I am not coming back. If I have to come back, then I didn't do my job right the first time and what good would it do to tell them the same message again? If I did do my job right, however, then they don't need me to come back.

Seriously, though, I don't think I'll be back. I can feel the passion and intensity of the burden slipping from me. All I want to do is go home.

But I have one more city to visit. Kisii is a small city a couple of hours away and I have three days of meetings there at two different churches. After almost two months out here, I'm almost done.

As I am pulling out of Kisumu in the early morning and I soak up the freshness of the air that has come after the rain last night, I am reminded that we are encouraged to cast our bread upon the waters, and it will come back to us. I have done that here. True, the water here may be muddy, but I have cast my bread out there, nonetheless.

Someday, who knows when it will come back to me in the form of churches revived and souls saved. That will make it all worthwhile.

"Cast thy bread upon the waters: for thou shalt find it after many days."
(Ecclesiastes 11:1)

A Final Match

Kisii is a small city nestled among the hills of western Kenya, not too far from Lake Victoria. I have been here twice before – once just passing through on my way to Tanzania, and the other to preach in a church here. This time I am scheduled for two days at a church that I have not been to before, but before I can leave Kisumu, another pastor in Kisii has been pleading for me to come to his church.

This happens a lot. They are hungry -- no,

starving -- for revival! We in America do not understand the depth of this hunger. We are more like the Church of Laodicea in our satisfied complacency.

This pastor has begged, pleaded, and entreated my host, Bishop Kibedi, to please squeeze them in somehow. But the only free day is the day off spent traveling to Kisii. That means hurry up and drive for 2 hours to Kisii, find a hotel somewhere and check-in, figure out where his church is, and get there by 10 am. [pant, pant]. Uh, I don't think so.

But he pleads that the people will wait no matter how long it takes me to get there. How do you refuse a request like that?

As it turns out, when I get there, it is a family church with a dozen members and a very young pastor who doesn't know what to do. There are no "60 people and many pastors", neither is it the 20-minute drive from Kisii like I was told. But hey, this is Africa, and everything is fluid here. Hakuna Matata, "no worries". Or as they are so fond of saying, "doan' warry". There is no "hurry" in Africa.

But this is what I do – go to the places no one else will go to and minister to those who have been overlooked or dismissed because it is not "cost-effective" to spend the time and money to reach them. I've been doing it for twelve years and one thing I have noticed is that when you reach down to minister to the "foolish things of the world", God always shows up. I guess that's just the way He is. He loves little children, widows, and orphans, lost causes, the weak and helpless, and little people. It is what He does.

The pastor from the main church that I am preaching in the next day is impressed. He realizes that the need is great for seasoned men and women of God to raise up these young pastors so that the flocks can be fed with the Word of God. As it is, even in the bigger churches, few people read the Bible. Some do, but most do not, so it is a small wonder that they are starving.

These last couple of days in this last church are

exhilarating. Maybe because the call to get home is so close that everything is ramped up for me. Maybe it's because I am giving one last great effort to ring the bell for revival before I make my final curtain call.

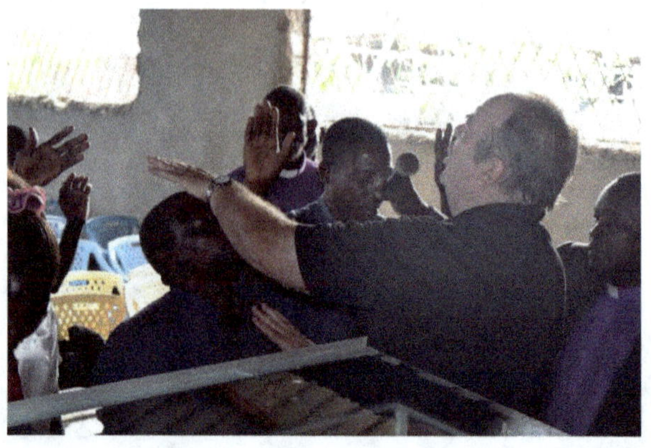

Whatever it is, the electricity runs wild. The people in this last church I am in not only "get it", but they have caught the fire and are already organizing the church to reading and prayer so they can be on fire when they head out into the streets to bring in the lost. I have told them the formula for revival and that once the Lord sees their faithfulness, He will begin to move.

They are not waiting; they are already on the march.

Jonathan – A Man of Vision

One of the messages that I have brought many times is the story in chapter 14 of 1st Samuel about Jonathan, the son of King Saul. It was one of the very first messages that the Lord brought to me about revival. Over time, it has grown to encompass messages about the necessity of the Word of God and prayer in bringing revival and the need for a vision for God.

King Saul had mustered 330,000 men of war to defeat the Philistines but then sent them all home after the victory except for 3,000 men. But guess what happens when you lay down your defenses. The enemy will attack. And that is what happened to Saul.

The Philistines came with more than a hundred thousand men, and the men of Israel fled to the caves and dens of the rocks. Only 600 men remained, but none of them had a sword. Only Saul and Jonathan had swords. What happened to all the swords? When we do not maintain our grasp of our sword, the Word of God, we lose our defense against the enemy.

But Jonathan was not like his father. He was a

man of vision for God. The circumstances around him did not matter. Jonathon did not look at how big the enemy was, but at how big his God was. Jonathan turned to his armor-bearer and said, *"…There is no restraint to the Lord to save by many or by few."* (1 Samuel 14:6)

And up the mountain, he went.

Jonathan climbed up that hill on his hands and knees, just as we must do battle on our knees with our hands clasped in prayer. At the top of that hill, as Jonathan wielded his sword, twenty men fell before him. That is the power of the Word of God when it is joined with the kind of prayer that contends all the way to the top of the mountain.

But that was not what made the revival break out. What did twenty men matter in the face of 100,000? What good would such a small effort do to bring down such overwhelming odds? Why bother with those little out-of-the-way churches with small congregations? How can God possibly use such puny things to spark a worldwide revival? I don't know. I just know He is God, and that's what He does.

God saw the faithfulness of a man who simply believed God and took hold of a vision for God that spurred him to action. Jonathan never looked at the situation around him, but he looked beyond the horizon to a God that was bigger than any problem and any army of the enemy. He had the courage to believe God. That courage drove him up that hill. Had he stayed at the bottom, nothing would have happened, and Israel would have been destroyed.

But when God saw that faithfulness, the earth began to quake, and the rocks began to fall, and the entire Philistine army began to run for their lives. They went down killing each other in their panic to flee.

And the Israelites that had run to hide in the caves? They came out and began to chase the enemy. In like manner, when real revival breaks out, all those

Christians that have run to the caves and dens to hide because of their discouragement with dead churches will suddenly see what they had been looking for in a newly revived outpouring of the Holy Ghost and will come forth.

This is the picture of revival that I see. It is not by might or by power but by the Spirit of God that revival will come. It is the little people of the Faith, not the big shots, which God will use to bring this great, end-time move of God just before Jesus comes back.

Revival is coming. But it is not coming to everybody. Only to those who answer the call and are willing to climb up that mountain, armed with the Word of God and the power of prayer. We need Jonathans with a vision to lead the way up that mountain so that God will shake the earth once more.

"But God hath chosen the foolish things of the world to confound the wise; and God hath chosen the weak things of the world to confound the things which are mighty."
(1 Corinthians 1:27)

Dawn

I've been listening to the reports of many of those whom I have ministered to as they begin to rise up and take their place as the Gideon Generation. The long-awaited harvest is beginning to grow up and break through the clods of fallow ground.

One young man in Kenya was full of zeal to start a church and become a pastor, but I had counseled him to go get a job instead. Start at the bottom and wait upon God. He did just that. It started with taking time during his break and praying with other members at his work. Then he began to stand up on the bus he was riding to work to witness to everyone on the bus. People got saved and encouraged. Then more people began doing the same and began to infiltrate the morning bus rides into a series of mobile churches. The prayer group began to grow and then spread. Now people from other companies are coming to the fellowship that takes place at his job. Even the bosses are beginning to promote it. There's no telling what can happen when a man allows God to do the growing.

Another brother had no church to go to, so he began to walk down a certain highway and simply speak a word to those that he found along the road. Soon people were expecting his daily ministering, and others came out looking for him. Just like the warmth of a morning sun, the glow from the Gospel is beginning to warm this previously ice-cold highway in Nairobi.

Then there are the testimonies from churches in Tanzania, Rwanda, Burundi, and Uganda of churches that have taken the message of revival to the streets because they were no longer content to sit idly by while the world slides off into Hell. Churches have doubled, tripled, and quadrupled. And where there was no church, churches have been planted. Thousands of souls have changed their eternal destination, hundreds have seen debilitating diseases washed away in the Blood of Jesus, and a countless number of poor people have been set free by Heaven-sent deliverances that have broken the shackles of Satan's demonic grip.

The ground has been broken up, the seeds planted and watered with tears, and slowly the harvest is beginning to break free from the confines of the earth. Revival is coming.

Home At Last

It's 5:30 in the morning. I can hear the birds outside singing and chirping to issue in this final day for me in Kenya. Tonight, I board my plane for home.

I woke up wishing that I could somehow make the world turn faster, zoom through the time that is left -- or even better, cancel out the rest of the day so I could get on that plane right now and sail off to home. I have been gone 6 weeks, and it has been a stretch. My girls have been texting me on the phone constantly just to reach a finger through the airwaves to touch Daddy, but it's never enough. But tonight, I am going home.

Each trip I have taken to Africa has been different. The message changes, the breadth and scope of the mission varies, and the intensity increases each time, but I have this hope that somehow everything is integrated into some grand plan that God has for Africa, and ultimately, the world. I may play a small part in His grand scheme, but even the greatest of forest fires can start with a single flame. I hope I have lit enough flames to start a fire in Kenya that will never be quenched.

At the end of each mission, I can't help

wondering if I accomplished that which the Lord had put before me to establish? Did I reach deep enough into their hearts? Was the Spirit of God flowing enough to transform them forever? Have souls been lit up and churches set on fire? Did we drive home the message deep enough into the hearts of these people? Did we light a fire of revival here hot enough to burn around the world?

We have given away hundreds of Bibles and preached to almost 40 churches. I have prayed over hundreds and hundreds of people, and I have seen the Spirit of God work miracles right before me. I have done what I have done and accomplished what I have accomplished. I have fought every battle that challenged me, and I drove home the Blood-Stained Banner of victory deep into the fertile soil of these people. It is now in their hands to grab hold of what God has offered them.

Even before I can get on the plane, pastors are calling to tell us how their churches have been energized and set on fire, how souls are filling up the church and getting saved like never before, and how thankful they are that their eyes have been opened to realize the calling that God has put before them to win souls and claim revival.

This trip was expensive, costing around $15,000, but in Heaven, we will see the eternal weight of what was purchased. Thank God for the handful of brothers and sisters who selflessly gave the finances to make it possible. Countless souls will seek you out in Eternity to thank you for your faith and generosity, and you will see the abundance of fruit that will be there because of you.

What is next for Africa? I believe that the fire will begin to grow and spread, and we will see something take place there that we have not seen in generations. I believe that the landscape of souls across this continent is so dry that once the fire is lit, it will become a blaze that nothing will be able to put out. It will burn so hot that we will feel the heat around the world.

But for me right now, however, all I can think about is getting home. My greatest reward will be to hug my girls and say, "Daddy is home!"

About the Author

Dalen Garris has been in ministry since 1970 during the Jesus Movement in California. In 1997, he began a radio broadcast that ultimately spread to dozens of countries, from Israel and Saudi Arabia to Africa and the Philippines. His program, *Fire in the Hole,* was selected for broadcast four times a week for several years across North America on the Sky Angel network as the Voice of Jerusalem.

A newspaper column followed, for which he has written over 700 articles, which have been published in local newspapers and Christian magazines in several countries. He has also written over a dozen books and several booklets.

Since 2004, he has been lighting the fires of revival in churches spread across sub-Saharan Africa. During the course of 17 years, he has preached in over 1,000 churches and has seen hundreds of them set on fire and explode with growth, and hundreds of new ones planted across Africa.

Hundreds of people have been supernaturally healed during the healing lines that so often sprang up during these revival meetings, and tens of thousands have been saved. And the fires are still burning.

Because of his work across Africa, Dalen Garris was awarded an honorary Doctorate in 2017 by the Northwestern Christian University of Florida.

Dr. Garris currently lives with Cindy, his wife of 43 years, in Waxahachie and is still heavily involved with churches across Africa.

His pressing hope is in seeing this powerful move of God in Africa ignite us here in America to see those same revival services that made such an explosion in Africa. He believes that this upcoming generation will be the Gideon Generation that will usher in this last, great revival that he has preached about for so many years.

Brother Dale, as he is known across Africa, has settled in Waxahachie, Texas, with his wife and three grown daughters and their children. You can contact him and find his pamphlets, books, videos, and podcasts at www.RevivalFire.org.

If you would like him to speak at your church or organization, please contact us for times and schedules.

He is willing to take this message anywhere people are hungry for a God-given, Holy Ghost revival.

Books by Dalen Garris:

Available at: www.Revivalfre.org/books

Four Steps to Revival

Do You Have Eternal Security?

Standing in the Gap

Two Covenants

Fire in the Hole

Revival Campaigns

The Kenya Diaries

A Trumpet in Nigeria

A Scent of Rain

Into the Heart of Darkness

Fire and Rain

Revival Campaigns in Africa – 2019

The Battle for Nigeria

A Light in the Bush

A Match in Dry Grass

A Voice in the Wilderness series:

vol. 1, The Journey Begins

vol. 2, the Early Years

vol. 3, Prophet Rising

vol. 4, Revival in the Wings

vol. 5, Sound of an Abundance of Rain

vol. 6, Watchman, What of the Night?

vol. 7, Mud and Heroes

vol. 8, Ashes in the Morning

vol. 9, Shaking the Olive Tree

vol. 10, Winds of Change

Booklets by Dalen Garris

- *Available at: www.Revivalfire.org/booklets/*

A Volcano in Cape Verde

Tanzania, 2011

Nigeria, 2012

Planting a Seed in Liberia

A Whisper in the Wind

Calvinism Critique

www.ingramcontent.com/pod-product-compliance
Lightning Source LLC
LaVergne TN
LVHW050542100826
845148LV00002B/650